SCHOLASTIC

3-Minute READING ASSESSMENTS

Word Recognition, Fluency, & Comprehension

Timothy V. Rasinski and Nancy Padak

Grades 1–4

New York • Toronto • London • Auckland • Sydney
Mexico City • New Delhi • Hong Kong • Buenos Aires

Teaching *Resources*

DEDICATION

We dedicate this book to a better understanding of how children read and to a renewed urgency to tailor instruction to meet children's individual needs in reading.

ACKNOWLEDGMENTS

We offer our deepest thanks to the teachers who helped and inspired us in the development and testing of this program. Most specifically our gratitude is extended to Betsey Shanahan, as well as the wonderful and dedicated teachers from the Canton City Schools (Canton, Ohio) and from Parkview Elementary in Wooster, Ohio.

We would also like to acknowledge Terry Cooper and Joanna Davis-Swing of Scholastic Inc., who have been instrumental in our being able to realize this project, and our editor, Merryl Maleska Wilbur, of Scholastic Inc., who helped us put all the pieces together.

Cover design by James Sarfati and Jason Robinson.
Cover photo by James Levin.
Interior design by Solutions by Design, Inc.

ISBN: 0-439-65089-5

Copyright © 2005 by Timothy V. Rasinski and Nancy Padak.
Published by Scholastic Inc.
All rights reserved.
Printed in the U.S.A.

20 21 22 23 24   40   21 20 19 18 17 16

Contents

Introduction

Assessment is a critical element of successful instruction. Assessment helps teachers determine if the instruction they provide students has resulted in adequate student progress. It allows teachers to identify students who can benefit from a more accelerated instructional program and those who need more intensive instructional intervention and support. And, if the assessment has sufficient precision, it allows teachers to identify a focus for their instruction. In a sense, assessment provides teachers (and schools and parents) with roadmaps that indicate where their children *are* academically, and where they need to go.

Research has indicated that assessment is critical to successful instruction. An international study of reading achievement, for example, found that regular assessment was a key factor associated with student success in learning to read (Postlethwaite & Ross, 1992).

In recent years, state and federal education mandates have required schools and school districts to more closely monitor student performance across a number of content areas and grade levels. These types of large-scale, typically norm-referenced assessments are most valuable for school administrators and policy makers in determining general trends in achievement and recommending policies and procedures at the national, state, and district levels for improving educational quality. For several reasons, however, these kinds of assessments cannot provide teachers with the information they need to make instructional decisions for individual students. One problem is timing—it frequently takes months for teachers to receive assessment results. In some cases a student has already moved on to the next grade before results are available. In addition, the scores on these tests do not lead naturally to instructional changes. Most often, scores simply tell whether or not a student has achieved "proficiency" rather than providing information about diagnostic needs or instructional direction.

Beyond the large-scale, general assessments that provide snapshots of achievement for a large number of children, a number of other reading assessments that lead to more precise instructional interventions are available. Some are commercial standardized tests such as the group-administered *Stanford Diagnostic Reading Test* and the individually administered *Woodcock Reading Mastery Test*. Others, such as informal reading inventories (IRIs) and running records (Clay, 1993) are more informal in nature and are based on teachers' ability to interpret the reading behaviors that they record. Still others, such as the *Developmental Reading Assessment* (Beaver, 1997) and the *Qualitative Reading Inventory* (Leslie & Caldwell, 2000) are hybrids of commercial standardized tests that include a strong informal, teacher-interpretation component. Most of these assessments provide teachers with an in-depth view of their students as readers— their level of achievement and, to some extent, their various strengths and areas of concern in reading.

If there is one major drawback to these sorts of assessments it is time. These and many of the other formal and informal reading assessments that are available to teachers take a considerable amount of time to prepare, administer, and score. The full-scale administration of an informal reading inventory, for example, can take one to two hours to give to a student and another hour (at least) to score and interpret. Although the data obtained from such an assessment are valid and valuable, the amount of time needed to administer such an assessment to every student in a classroom is prohibitive.

Nevertheless, we are seeing instances in many schools in which teachers are expected to administer an informal reading inventory to every child in their classrooms two, and in some cases three, times per year. In a classroom of 25 children, three administrations of an IRI, even if each required only one hour per child, would take 75 hours—the equivalent of nearly three full weeks of school!

Time for Assessment or Time for Instruction?

As valuable as assessment is for teachers, it is in instruction where the rubber meets the road. Students learn as a result of instruction, not assessment. While assessment most certainly must guide instruction, it is no substitute for it. And in schools and classrooms where inordinate amounts of time are taken for assessment, an equal amount of time is taken *from* instruction. In short, time given to assessment is time taken away from instruction. The irony of the situation is that the very thing that assessment is intended to measure—achievement—is curtailed by the time that must be taken away from instruction in order to do the assessment. The 50 hours that it might take to administer an informal reading inventory to every child in a classroom, for example, could have been used to provide reading instruction that would have made those students better readers!

Advantages of *3-Minute Reading Assessments*

With the above considerations in mind, we developed this set of assessments to provide classroom teachers and specialists with a quick way to obtain valid diagnostic information about students' reading achievement. In fewer than five minutes, you can use this system to measure a child's progress and identify areas of strength and concern that may need special and intensive instruction. You will be able to sample a student's reading and determine his or her level of performance in three critical areas—word recognition (decoding), reading fluency, and comprehension. The information obtained from *3-Minute Reading Assessments: Word Recognition, Fluency, and Comprehension* will enable you to monitor student progress over time across these three dimensions of reading, identify areas of special need for individual children, and communicate to parents and others about student progress in reading.

Use *3-Minute Reading Assessments* Throughout the Year

We recommend that you use *3-Minute Reading Assessments* with an individual student three or four times per year at regular intervals—once at the beginning of the school year, once or twice in the middle of the year, and once at the end of the year. You should be able to assess and score a classroom of 25 students in about two hours. Since we've provided four forms for each grade, you will be able to use a different, but equivalent form for each assessment throughout the year.

By assessing students at regular times during the school year you will be able to measure progress in word recognition, reading fluency, and comprehension over the course of the year. You will be able to identify students who are not responding well to your instructional efforts. This will allow you to plan additional or more targeted instruction for those students who are struggling or who are not demonstrating the kind of progress you hope to see.

What's Included in *3-Minute Reading Assessments*

In addition to the background discussion above, this Introduction provides you with a full set of specific directions for administering these assessments. Immediately following those directions we provide scoring and interpretation guides for each of the three major areas covered by the assessments (note that fluency is assessed in *two* distinct dimensions—fluency-automaticity and fluency-expression). Included are

1. the procedure for calculating **word recognition accuracy**,

2. a chart for measuring **fluency through reading rate**,

3. a scale for figuring **fluency through expression**, and

4. a rubric for determining **comprehension**.

In addition to these fully detailed guides (pages 9–12), you'll also find a condensed version of all four guides on page 58. This page is intended to offer you a handy aid that can be torn out and laminated for use during the administration of each passage. We hope it will give you an easy reference point as you listen to the student's reading.

The passages themselves are divided into four grade-level booklets. Each booklet includes the four equivalent forms (A through D) mentioned above. To vary subject matter and maintain interest, the forms are organized by themes: Form A passages pertain to family outings; Form B passages to foods; Form C passages to extreme weather; and Form D to unique individuals. For each form there is a student page, which includes the passage only and is intended for direct use with the student, and an accompanying teacher page. The teacher page reproduces the passage and gives you additional information, such as overall word count and the word length of each printed line. In addition, at the bottom of each teacher page, a scoring section enables you to jot down the student's scores as you figure them, as well as any additional comments.

We strongly recommend recording the data yielded by the assessments, and to make keeping these records easy, we provide two different recording charts. On page 56, you'll find a class record sheet and on page 57, an individual student record sheet. The former enables you to get an overview of class performance at a glance, while the latter helps you track testing data for all four forms for an individual student. You may wish to use both, or simply choose the one that best fits your needs. These charts allow you to highlight areas where performance is below your expectations as well as areas with no growth over time. You may want to address these areas with additional assessment and instruction and bring them to the attention of parents, school administrators, or other teachers.

In order to help you address targeted areas of concern, we include a brief section of Instructional Ideas for each of the three major areas assessed. Pages 59–63 offer instructional suggestions for teaching word recognition, fluency, and comprehension skills. Of course, these ideas are just a springboard for each topic. Entire books of instruction for each area are available!

A Word About Readability Determination

As described above, four different passages for each grade level are presented in separate grade-level booklets. We have spent considerable time checking the readability of these passages before designating each to be at a specific grade level. In doing so, we applied either all or several of the following formulas: the Flesch Reading Ease Formula; the Flesch-Kincaid Grade Level Formula; the Fry Readability Graph; the Spache Readability Formula; and the Dale-Chall Readability Formula. As well, we tapped our own expertise as professors of literacy and researchers to level the passages.

In the end, readability is often a matter of judgment. It is well known that readability results will vary depending on which formula is used and that each formula has its own limitations and drawbacks. That said, there are currently no better alternatives that offer a more accurate or efficient approach to determining grade level for a particular reading passage. Thus, with all this in mind, we feel confident in stating that these passages are on grade level and are equivalent, within each form, in terms of difficulty.

A few additional notes about grade levels and the way we've set up these assessments: We recommend having students read passages at their assigned school-year grade levels because this will help you determine their level of performance on passages that they are expected to master during that school year. In other words, while one third grader may be reading comfortably at fourth-grade level and another at second-grade level, this assessment enables you to determine how well both students will be able to read the grade-level texts you use for instruction. Students whose grade-level performance is excellent may not need repeated assessment. Those who struggle with the grade-level passage will need additional diagnosis. Retesting these students on grade-level test passages throughout the school year will easily allow you to gauge their growth.

Directions for Administering *3-Minute Reading Assessments*

Administering these assessments is simple and straightforward. You simply ask students to read a grade-level passage to you and ask them to recall what they remember from the passage after they've read it. While students read and recall the passage, you monitor their performance for word recognition, fluency, and comprehension. Specific directions are outlined below:

1. Present the student with a copy of the passage from *3-Minute Reading Assessments* that corresponds to his assigned grade level. Ask the student to read the passage orally to you in the way he might normally read the passage. Tell the student that at the end of the reading you will ask him to tell you what he remembers about the passage.

2. The student reads the passage aloud for 60 seconds. If she stops at an unknown word and does not attempt to pronounce it for 2 seconds, or if she attempts the word but clearly has little chance of reading it correctly, tell her the word and ask her to continue reading. During the oral reading, keep your copy of the passage in front of you. Mark any uncorrected errors that the student makes by drawing a line through the missed word. Errors include words that are mispronounced or that you provide to the student and words that the student omits. If a student initially mispronounces or omits a word, but corrects it, write and circle a *c* above the word to indicate it was corrected (and do not count these corrected words as errors). At the end of the 60-second period, mark the point the student has reached in her reading of the text.

3. After the student has read for 60 seconds, direct his attention to the beginning of the text and ask him to follow along silently while you read the text aloud. Read the passage to the child in a normal and expressive voice. (We ask that you read the text to the student to remove any difficulties he may have had in word recognition or fluency that could hamper his comprehension of the passage. Listening comprehension is a good measure of the students' reading comprehension [Biemiller, 2003].)

4. At the end of your reading, remove the passage from the student's view and ask her to tell you what she remembers from the passage. After she has retold the passage, ask her if there is anything else she remembers about what she read. If the student is unable or unwilling to retell anything at all from the passage, you may ask for specific information (for example, "What is the main idea of this story?" or "What was described in this story?").

Note: If the student has made few oral reading errors and has not reached the end of the passage within 60 seconds, you may, as an alternative to reading the passage to the student, ask him to read the balance of the passage silently. At the end of the student's reading, remove the passage from view and ask him to retell what he remembers from the reading. Keep in mind, however, that a source of any difficulty in comprehension may be subtle or undetected problems in word recognition or fluency.

After the student has retold the passage, the assessment is complete.

Scoring and Interpreting the Assessment

Scoring *3-Minute Reading Assessments* is simple and quick. The following procedures should be followed:

Word Recognition Accuracy (Decoding)

Word recognition is determined by calculating the percentage of words read correctly in the 60-second oral reading. Divide the number of words read correctly by the total number of words read (correctly *or* incorrectly). For example, if the student read a total of 94 words in the 60-second reading and made 8 errors, the percentage of words read correctly would be reflected in the following fraction:

$$\frac{86}{94} \text{ (86 divided by 94)} = 91.5\%$$

In other words, the student read 91.5 percent of the words correctly.

Instructional reading level is normally marked by a word recognition accuracy rate of 92–98 percent. Independent reading level is normally marked by an accuracy rate of 99–100 percent.

A normally developing student should begin the school year reading grade-level material at an instructional level and, by the end of the school year, at an independent word recognition level. For example, a third grader's performance on a third-grade passage would be instructional at the beginning of the year but independent by the end of the year. Students who perform at the frustration level at the end of the school year, or who do not demonstrate good progress over the year, should be considered for additional assessment to confirm their decoding difficulty. Such students may benefit from specific instructional intervention in decoding (see pages 59–60).

Note that the above progression does not apply to first grade. Although first graders should be able to read first-grade material with 99–100 percent accuracy at the end of grade one, no expectations should be made for the first six months of grade one. During this period, students are just gaining initial decoding skills and should not be expected to decode first-grade material at an instructional or independent level.

Reading Fluency-Automaticity

One way reading fluency can be measured is through reading rate. Reading rate provides a measure of the extent to which a reader can automatically decode words, thus leaving cognitive resources free for the more important task of comprehending a passage. To determine rate, simply count the number of words the student has read correctly during the 60-second oral read. Words read correctly include those words that were initially misread but corrected by the student. Then, using the appropriate grade level and time period, compare the student's performance against the reading rates shown on page 10.

A student whose reading rate falls within the appropriate range shown above is performing at grade-level expectations. Students who fall below the range may be considered at-risk in terms of fluency-automaticity. Additional assessment may be

TARGET READING RATES BY GRADE LEVEL

Grade	Fall wcpm*	Winter wcpm	Spring wcpm
1	0–10	10–50	30–90
2	30–80	50–100	70–130
3	50–110	70–120	80–140
4	70–120	80–130	90–140
5	80–130	90–140	100–150
6	90–140	100–150	110–160
7	100–150	110–160	120–170
8	110–160	120–180	130–180

*wcpm=words correct per minute

appropriate for students who perform poorly at the end of the school year or who do not show improvement over the course of the year. These students may benefit from instruction aimed at improving reading fluency (see page 60). Students whose reading rate is above the range limits may be considered to be performing well in fluency-automaticity. However, an important caveat must be noted: Students who read exceptionally fast without attending to punctuation and other phrase boundaries, and who read without sufficient expression may also be considered at-risk in fluency. The following assessment for fluency-expression should be used with all students to give you the fullest picture of a student's fluency skills.

Reading Fluency-Expression

Reading fluency is more than just reading fast. It is also the ability to interpret a text with appropriate phrasing and expression. You can measure this dimension of fluency by listening to the student's 60-second oral reading and rating it on the Multidimensional Fluency Scale (see page 11). Initially you may need to tape record the student's reading and listen to it in order to provide a rating for each of the four scales. Soon, however, you will be able to score the scales on the spot.

At the beginning of the school year, it is not unusual for students to score in the bottom half of each of the fluency dimensions (i.e., to have a total fluency score of 8 or below). However, by the end of the school year, students should be rated in the top half in each dimension when they are reading grade-level material (i.e., they should be able to achieve a total fluency score of 9 or above). End-of-year ratings in the bottom half for any of the fluency dimensions, or a total fluency score of 8 or less, may indicate a need for additional assessment or instructional intervention (see pages 60–61). The Multi-dimensional Fluency Scale is also useful for helping students evaluate their own reading and in developing their own understanding of fluency in reading.

MULTIDIMENSIONAL FLUENCY SCALE

Rating	Expression & Volume	Phrasing and Intonation	Smoothness	Pace
Circle one →	1 2 3 4	1 2 3 4	1 2 3 4	1 2 3 4
1	Reads words as if simply to get them out. Little sense of trying to make text sound like natural language. Tends to read in a quiet voice.	Reads in monotone with little sense of phrase boundaries; frequently reads word-by-word.	Makes frequent extended pauses, hesitations, false starts, sound-outs, repetitions, and/or multiple attempts.	Reads slowly and laboriously.
2	Begins to use voice to make text sound like natural language in some areas but not in others. Focus remains largely on pronouncing the words. Still reads in a quiet voice.	Frequently reads in two- and three-word phrases, giving the impression of choppy reading; improper stress and intonation fail to mark ends of sentences and clauses.	Experiences several "rough spots" in text where extended pauses or hesitations are more frequent and disruptive.	Reads moderately slowly or too quickly.
3	Makes text sound like natural language throughout the better part of the passage. Occasionally slips into expressionless reading. Voice volume is generally appropriate throughout the text.	Reads with a mixture of run-ons, mid-sentence pauses for breath, and some choppiness; reasonable stress and intonation.	Occasionally breaks smooth rhythm because of difficulties with specific words and/or structures.	Reads with an uneven mixture of fast and slow pace.
4	Reads with good expression and enthusiasm throughout the text. Varies expression and volume to match his or her interpretation of the passage.	Generally reads with good phrasing, mostly in clause and sentence units.	Generally reads smoothly with some breaks, but resolves word and structure difficulties quickly, usually through self-correction.	Consistently reads at conversational pace; appropriate rate throughout reading.

* This scale is an adaptation of one developed by Zutell & Rasinski, 1991.
Kimberly Monfort, a third-grade teacher at Bon View School in Ontario, California developed the format above for the scale.

Total Score: _____

Comprehension

How well students understand what they read is the ultimate hallmark of proficient reading. You can get a good sense of a student's ability to understand a text through the retelling. When you are satisfied that a student has told you as much as he or she can remember from the passage, rate the recall on the Comprehension Rubric (see page 12). As mentioned in the Directions for Administering section, under some circumstances you may wish to have the student himself or herself read the balance of the passage silently. Use the same comprehension rubric to score the retelling whether you read the passage aloud to the student or whether you allow the student to read the passage silently.

A score of 3 or below suggests inadequate recall and comprehension of the passage. At the beginning of the school year, it is not unusual for a student's recall of a grade-level passage to be rated at level 3 or below. By the end of the school year, student performance should be in the upper half of the scale (levels 4–6). Scores in the lower half of the scale at the end of the year should signal the need for a more in-depth diagnosis and perhaps instructional intervention in comprehension. See pages 61–63 for suggested instructional ideas to use with students who may have comprehension difficulties.

COMPREHENSION RUBRIC

◇ Student has no recall or minimal recall of only a fact or two from the passage. **Rating Score: 1**

◇ Student recalls a number of unrelated facts of varied importance. **Rating Score: 2**

◇ Student recalls the main idea of the passage with a few supporting details. **Rating Score: 3**

◇ Student recalls the main idea along with a fairly robust set of supporting details, although not necessarily organized logically or sequentially as presented in the passage. **Rating Score: 4**

◇ Student recall is a comprehensive summary of the passage, presented in a logical order and/or with a robust set of details, and includes a statement of main idea. **Rating Score: 5**

◇ Student recall is a comprehensive summary of the passage, presented in a logical order and/or with a robust set of details, and includes a statement of main idea. Student also makes reasonable connections beyond the text, such as to his/her own personal life or another text. **Rating Score: 6**

Test Passages

GRADE 1 BOOKLET:
Student Passages and Teacher Pages

We went to the park. My mom and dad took me. I had so much fun. The park was big. There was a lot to do. I went on the swings first. I flew high in the air. My mom said not to go so high. I told her birds fly higher than me.

Then we went on the slide. It was the little one. My dad went on with me. My mom said he looked silly. I thought so, too. I was afraid of the big slide. It was too big. My mom and dad went on it. I was still afraid.

We fed the ducks. All the ducks quacked. They sounded like car horns. Then my mom and dad sat. I played in the sand. It was a great day. I want to go again.

Name of student _____ Date of testing _____

Grade 1: Form A

We went to the park. My	6
mom and dad took me. I had	13
so much fun. The park was big.	20
There was a lot to do. I went	28
on the swings first. I flew high in	36
the air. My mom said not to go	44
so high. I told her birds fly	51
higher than me.	54
Then we went on the slide.	60
It was the little one. My dad	67
went on with me. My mom	73
said he looked silly. I thought	79
so, too. I was afraid of the big	87
slide. It was too big. My mom	94
and dad went on it. I was still	102
afraid.	103
We fed the ducks. All the	109
ducks quacked. They sounded	113
like car horns. Then my mom	119
and dad sat. I played in the	126
sand. It was a great day. I	133
want to go again.	137

Word Count – 137

Scoring

Word recognition accuracy:

$$\frac{\text{Words correct}}{\text{Total words read orally}} = _____ = _____ \%$$

Fluency-Automaticity: _____ wcpm

Multidimensional Fluency Scale

Expression and Volume: _____

Phrasing and Intonation: _____

Smoothness: _____

Pace: _____

Total Score: _____

Comprehension: _____

Comments and Observations:

I love hot dogs. They are the best food. They taste good. I eat them all the time. I eat them for lunch. Sometimes I eat them for dinner, too.

Hot dogs are warm and tasty. I like them in a bun. The buns look like boats. I like ketchup on my hot dogs. It makes them taste so good. My dad eats hot dogs, too. He does not like buns. He says the hot dog has no coat on.

My dad cooks hot dogs outside. They are crisp. My mother cooks them indoors. Hot dogs cooked indoors are soft. I like them both ways.

I take little bites of my hot dogs. I like to make them last. I love hot dogs.

Name of student _____ Date of testing _____

Grade 1: Form B

I love hot dogs. They are	6
the best food. They taste	11
good. I eat them all the time. I	19
eat them for lunch. Sometimes	24
I eat them for dinner, too.	30
Hot dogs are warm and	35
tasty. I like them in a bun. The	43
buns look like boats. I like	49
ketchup on my hot dogs. It	55
makes them taste so good.	60
My dad eats hot dogs, too.	66
He does not like buns. He says	73
the hot dog has no coat on.	80
My dad cooks hot dogs	85
outside. They are crisp. My	90
mother cooks them indoors.	94
Hot dogs cooked indoors are	99
soft. I like them both ways.	105
I take little bites of my hot	112
dogs. I like to make them last.	119
I love hot dogs.	123

Word Count – 123

Scoring

Word recognition accuracy:

$$\frac{\text{Words correct}}{\text{Total words read orally}} = \text{_____} = \text{_____} \%$$

Fluency-Automaticity: _____ wcpm

Multidimensional Fluency Scale

  Expression and Volume: _____

  Phrasing and Intonation: _____

  Smoothness: _____

  Pace: _____

  Total Score: _____

Comprehension: _____

Comments and Observations:

It is hot. The sun is out. I am very hot. Mother said I should play outside. It is too hot to play ball. It is too hot to ride bikes. It is way too hot to run around. I do not know what to do.

I want to get cool. I want to swim, but the pool is closed. We can't swim until the pool is open. I try sitting under the tree. It is even hot under the tree. The grass is hot. It makes me itch. There is nothing to do under the tree.

I am going to go in the house. The air is cool in there. Soon we can go to the pool. It is too hot to play.

Name of student _____ Date of testing _____

Grade 1: Form C

It is hot. The sun is out. I am	9
very hot. Mother said I should	15
play outside. It is too hot to	22
play ball. It is too hot to ride	30
bikes. It is way too hot to run	38
around. I do not know what	44
to do.	46
I want to get cool. I want to	54
swim, but the pool is closed.	60
We can't swim until the pool is	67
open. I try sitting under the	73
tree. It is even hot under the	80
tree. The grass is hot. It makes	87
me itch. There is nothing to do	94
under the tree.	97
I am going to go in the	104
house. The air is cool in there.	111
Soon we can go to the pool. It	119
is too hot to play.	124

Word Count – 124

Scoring	
Word recognition accuracy:	Comments and Observations:
$\dfrac{\text{Words correct}}{\text{Total words read orally}}$ = _____ = _____ %	
Fluency-Automaticity: _____ wcpm	
Multidimensional Fluency Scale	
Expression and Volume: _____	
Phrasing and Intonation: _____	
Smoothness: _____	
Pace: _____	
Total Score: _____	
Comprehension: _____	

I love my mother. She is very nice. She loves me, too. My mother is tall. She has red hair. She smiles all the time. She is very happy.

I like to read with my mother. She reads to me before I go to bed. She likes books about dogs. I like books about cats. We take turns picking the books.

My mother also likes to hug. She hugs me all the time. I like it most of the time. I do not like it when she hugs me at school. She calls me her baby cakes.

Then my friends laugh. I tell her to stop, but I am not mad.

My mother is never late. She picks me up after school every day. She always has a good snack to eat. She is the best.

Name of student _____ Date of testing _____

Grade 1: Form D

I love my mother. She is very	7
nice. She loves me, too. My	13
mother is tall. She has red hair.	20
She smiles all the time. She is	27
very happy.	29
I like to read with my	35
mother. She reads to me	40
before I go to bed. She likes	47
books about dogs. I like books	53
about cats. We take turns	58
picking the books.	61
My mother also likes to hug.	67
She hugs me all the time. I like	75
it most of the time. I do not like	84
it when she hugs me at school.	91
She calls me her baby cakes.	97
Then my friends laugh. I tell her	104
to stop, but I am not mad.	111
My mother is never late.	116
She picks me up after school	122
every day. She always has a	128
good snack to eat. She is the	135
best.	136

Word Count – 136

Scoring

Word recognition accuracy:

$$\frac{\text{Words correct}}{\text{Total words read orally}} = \underline{\hspace{1.5cm}} = \underline{\hspace{1.5cm}} \%$$

Fluency-Automaticity: _____ wcpm

Multidimensional Fluency Scale

Expression and Volume: _____

Phrasing and Intonation: _____

Smoothness: _____

Pace: _____

Total Score: _____

Comprehension: _____

Comments and Observations:

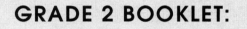

Test Passages

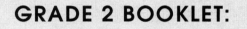

GRADE 2 BOOKLET:

Student Passages and Teacher Pages

This weekend I went to the zoo. It was awesome. I went with my mom and dad. My sister came, too. The zoo was in the city. It took a long time to drive there. My sister and I complained a lot. My dad said we sounded like broken records.

When we got there, I was excited. I wanted to see the seals first. I loved the seals. They put on a show. The seals could balance balls on their noses. I clapped so hard my hands turned red. They looked like they had a sunburn. Next we went to see the lions. They were just lying around. My sister called them "lazy bones." My mom wanted to see the monkeys. She says my sister and I remind her of them. The monkeys were cool. They were swinging on ropes the way I do at recess.

Then we got ice cream. It tasted so good I could have eaten a lot more. My trip to the zoo was super.

Name of student _____ Date of testing _____

Grade 2: Form A

This weekend I went to the zoo. It was	9
awesome. I went with my mom and dad.	17
My sister came, too. The zoo was in the	26
city. It took a long time to drive there. My	36
sister and I complained a lot. My dad	44
said we sounded like broken records.	50
When we got there, I was excited. I	58
wanted to see the seals first. I loved the	67
seals. They put on a show. The seals	75
could balance balls on their noses. I	82
clapped so hard my hands turned red.	89
They looked like they had a sunburn.	96
Next we went to see the lions. They were	105
just lying around. My sister called them	112
"lazy bones." My mom wanted to see the	120
monkeys. She says my sister and I remind	128
her of them. The monkeys were cool.	135
They were swinging on ropes the way I	143
do at recess.	146
Then we got ice cream. It tasted so	154
good I could have eaten a lot more. My	163
trip to the zoo was super.	169

Word Count – 169

Scoring

Word recognition accuracy:

$$\frac{\text{Words correct}}{\text{Total words read orally}} = \underline{\hspace{2cm}} = \underline{\hspace{2cm}} \%$$

Fluency-Automaticity: _____ wcpm

Multidimensional Fluency Scale
   Expression and Volume: _____
   Phrasing and Intonation: _____
   Smoothness: _____
   Pace: _____
   Total Score: _____

Comprehension: _____

Comments and Observations:

Do you like apples? I think apples are great. They are a fun fruit to eat. Apples come in many colors. They can be red or green. They can be yellow or pink. Most apples are sweet. Some are not. I like the sweet ones best.

Apples make a crunchy sound when you bite them. Apples are juicy. The juice runs out of my mouth when I take a bite. It goes down my chin and makes me sticky.

You can eat apples whole, or you can eat them in slices. Apples can be in pies. I like to eat apples in all sorts of things.

I like to pick apples, too. Apples grow on trees. They are like presents on a branch. They are just waiting to be opened. Eating apples is fun to do. They are good for you, too.

Name of student _____ Date of testing _____

Grade 2: Form B

Do you like apples? I think apples	7
are great. They are a fun fruit to eat.	16
Apples come in many colors. They can	23
be red or green. They can be yellow or	32
pink. Most apples are sweet. Some are	39
not. I like the sweet ones best.	46
Apples make a crunchy sound	51
when you bite them. Apples are juicy.	58
The juice runs out of my mouth when I	67
take a bite. It goes down my chin and	76
makes me sticky.	79
You can eat apples whole, or you	86
can eat them in slices. Apples can be	94
in pies. I like to eat apples in all sorts of	105
things.	106
I like to pick apples, too. Apples	113
grow on trees. They are like presents	120
on a branch. They are just waiting to	128
be opened. Eating apples is fun to do.	136
They are good for you, too.	142

Word Count – 142

Scoring	

Word recognition accuracy:

$$\frac{\text{Words correct}}{\text{Total words read orally}} = _____ = _____ \%$$

Fluency-Automaticity: _____ wcpm

Multidimensional Fluency Scale

Expression and Volume: _____

Phrasing and Intonation: _____

Smoothness: _____

Pace: _____

Total Score: _____

Comprehension: _____

Comments and Observations:

It is so cold today! I went for a walk with my dog, and it was freezing. When I went outside, the air hurt my eyes. My eyes were filled with tears, but I was not crying. My ears hurt, too. The cold air made them feel like ice cubes in the freezer. I could hear bells ringing, but there were no bells.

I did not wear gloves even though my mother told me to. My fingers got so cold they felt hot. What a surprise to feel so cold that you begin to feel hot! My body was not cold. I had a big coat on that kept me as warm as when I am snuggled up in bed.

My dog was cold, too. She kept pulling on her leash to go back to the house. Our walk was not very long. I don't like it when it is this cold. My dog does not like it, either.

Name of student _____ Date of testing _____

Grade 2: Form C

It is so cold today! I went for a walk	10
with my dog, and it was freezing.	17
When I went outside, the air hurt my	25
eyes. My eyes were filled with tears,	32
but I was not crying. My ears hurt, too.	41
The cold air made them feel like ice	49
cubes in the freezer. I could hear bells	57
ringing, but there were no bells.	63
I did not wear gloves even though	70
my mother told me to. My fingers got	78
so cold they felt hot. What a surprise to	87
feel so cold that you begin to feel hot!	96
My body was not cold. I had a big	105
coat on that kept me as warm as	113
when I am snuggled up in bed.	120
My dog was cold, too. She kept	127
pulling on her leash to go back to the	136
house. Our walk was not very long. I	144
don't like it when it is this cold. My dog	154
does not like it, either.	159

Word Count – 159

Scoring

Word recognition accuracy:

$$\frac{\text{Words correct}}{\text{Total words read orally}} = \underline{\hspace{1cm}} = \underline{\hspace{1cm}} \%$$

Fluency-Automaticity: _____ wcpm

Multidimensional Fluency Scale

  Expression and Volume: _____

  Phrasing and Intonation: _____

  Smoothness: _____

  Pace: _____

  Total Score: _____

Comprehension: _____

Comments and Observations:

I have an awesome dad. He is the best dad in the world. My dad is tall and strong like a football player. He can carry my sister and me at the same time. It is really fun when he does that. He pretends that he is a monster, and he chases us. When we get caught, he puts us on the couch. We pretend that is our cage.

My dad is very funny. He makes a lot of jokes and is silly. My mom says he is a clown and always has been. I like it when he acts silly. It is like going to the circus, but we are at home. My dad likes to play with me a lot. He can play football like a pro. I want to be just like my dad.

Name of student _____ Date of testing _____

Grade 2: Form D

I have an awesome dad. He is the	8
best dad in the world. My dad is tall	17
and strong like a football player. He	24
can carry my sister and me at the	32
same time. It is really fun when he	40
does that. He pretends that he is a	48
monster, and he chases us. When we	55
get caught, he puts us on the couch.	63
We pretend that is our cage.	69
My dad is very funny. He makes a	77
lot of jokes and is silly. My mom says he	87
is a clown and always has been. I like	96
it when he acts silly. It is like going to	106
the circus, but we are at home. My	114
dad likes to play with me a lot. He can	124
play football like a pro. I want to be	133
just like my dad.	137

Word Count – 137

Scoring

Word recognition accuracy:

$$\frac{\text{Words correct}}{\text{Total words read orally}} = \text{_____} = \text{_____} \%$$

Fluency-Automaticity: _____ wcpm

Multidimensional Fluency Scale
  Expression and Volume: _____
  Phrasing and Intonation: _____
  Smoothness: _____
  Pace: _____
  Total Score: _____

Comprehension: _____

Comments and Observations:

Test Passages

GRADE 3 BOOKLET:
Student Passages and Teacher Pages

Family trips can be fun, but some are not. Last month my family went to the beach, but I did not have a very good time. The drive took ten hours in the car. Those ten hours felt like ten days. It was plain torture. When we arrived, the house looked like it hadn't been lived in for several years. The paint on the house was peeling off in little yellow flakes. In fact, it looked like the house was painted in sticky notes. The stairs to the front door shook when you stepped on them, as if you were walking on a boat in a storm. I had to share a room with my little sister, which was awful.

The weather was the worst part of the trip. Every day during the entire week was overcast. The skies looked like the gray of our garage floor. It rained day and night, and so we had to stay inside. We did walk down to the beach a couple of times. One day it was so windy I felt like I was a kite being blown around the beach. The sand whipped through the air and stung our faces like tiny bees.

We had fun a few times. My dad and I went for a walk on the beach, and I found a hermit crab on the jetty. That was really cool. Next year when we go to the beach I will be hoping for better weather.

Name of student _____ Date of testing _____

Grade 3: Form A

Family trips can be fun, but some are not.	9
Last month my family went to the beach, but I	19
did not have a very good time. The drive took	29
ten hours in the car. Those ten hours felt like ten	40
days. It was plain torture. When we arrived, the	49
house looked like it hadn't been lived in for	58
several years. The paint on the house was	66
peeling off in little yellow flakes. In fact, it looked	76
like the house was painted in sticky notes. The	85
stairs to the front door shook when you stepped	94
on them, as if you were walking on a boat in a	106
storm. I had to share a room with my little sister,	117
which was awful.	120
The weather was the worst part of the trip.	129
Every day during the entire week was overcast.	137
The skies looked like the gray of our garage floor.	147
It rained day and night, and so we had to stay	158
inside. We did walk down to the beach a couple	168
of times. One day it was so windy I felt like I was	181
a kite being blown around the beach. The sand	190
whipped through the air and stung our faces like	199
tiny bees.	201
We had fun a few times. My dad and I went	212
for a walk on the beach, and I found a hermit	223
crab on the jetty. That was really cool. Next year	233
when we go to the beach I will be hoping for	244
better weather.	246

Word Count – 246

Scoring

Word recognition accuracy:

$$\frac{\text{Words correct}}{\text{Total words read orally}} = \text{_____} = \text{_____} \%$$

Fluency-Automaticity: _____ wcpm

Multidimensional Fluency Scale

   Expression and Volume: _____

   Phrasing and Intonation: _____

   Smoothness: _____

   Pace: _____

   Total Score: _____

Comprehension: _____

Comments and Observations:

Milk is a very nice drink to drink. It is cold and refreshing and tastes delicious. Milk is white like brand-new snow. It is white like a kitten named Snowball. Milk is white like a marshmallow waiting to be cooked over a fire. Milk is a smooth and silky drink. It slides down your throat like water in a stream. The cold liquid fills your mouth with a cool feeling—like eating mint candy.

Milk is full of vitamins and minerals that are good for you. With each swallow, you feel like your bones are getting stronger. Your teeth feel like they are getting whiter. Milk tastes fresh. It tastes like morning dew on newly mowed grass.

Milk is good with other things, too. I love dipping cookies into milk, mixing it with ice cream, or pouring it on cereal. My mom says that I have to drink my milk at dinner. She doesn't know that this is an extra treat for me. Don't tell her my secret; it is just between you and me.

■ GRADE 3

40   *3-Minute Reading Assessments: Word Recognition, Fluency, and Comprehension—Grades 1–4* Scholastic Teaching Resources

Name of student _____ Date of testing _____

Grade 3: Form B

Milk is a very nice drink to drink. It is cold	11
and refreshing and tastes delicious. Milk is	18
white like brand-new snow. It is white like a	27
kitten named Snowball. Milk is white like a	35
marshmallow waiting to be cooked over a	42
fire. Milk is a smooth and silky drink. It slides	52
down your throat like water in a stream. The	61
cold liquid fills your mouth with a cool	69
feeling—like eating mint candy.	74
Milk is full of vitamins and minerals that	82
are good for you. With each swallow, you	90
feel like your bones are getting stronger.	97
Your teeth feel like they are getting whiter.	105
Milk tastes fresh. It tastes like morning dew	113
on newly mowed grass.	117
Milk is good with other things, too. I love	126
dipping cookies into milk, mixing it with ice	134
cream, or pouring it on cereal. My mom	142
says that I have to drink my milk at dinner.	152
She doesn't know that this is an extra treat	161
for me. Don't tell her my secret; it is just	171
between you and me.	175

Word Count – 175

Scoring

Word recognition accuracy:

Words correct / Total words read orally = _____ = _____ %

Fluency-Automaticity: _____ wcpm

Multidimensional Fluency Scale

Expression and Volume: _____

Phrasing and Intonation: _____

Smoothness: _____

Pace: _____

Total Score: _____

Comprehension: _____

Comments and Observations:

GRADE 3

3-Minute Reading Assessments: Word Recognition, Fluency, and Comprehension—Grades 1–4 Scholastic Teaching Resources **41**

When I was playing today at recess, I felt like a kite blown around by the wind. It was hard to stay in one place because the wind pushed me from here to there. It was like being a yo-yo on a string, going back and forth. Each time I thought I was safe, another gust blew me off in another direction. My friends were trying to play kickball, but the ball kept blowing away. It was like a funny movie.

The teachers were not happy, either. They were all together in a bunch, trying to keep their hair neat. Mr. Lewis wasn't with the other teachers; he was pushing the girls on the swings. It was an easy job since the wind did most of the work.

My sister was out at recess, too. She and her friend Mary were trying to write a play but their papers kept blowing away. I tried to help her catch them, but it was hard. We got all the pieces, so we didn't litter, but the pages were ruined. My sister and Mary decided to chase me instead of writing, and we had a great time. We were blown from here to there and it was fun.

Name of student _____ Date of testing _____

Grade 3: Form C

When I was playing today at recess,	7
I felt like a kite blown around by the wind.	17
It was hard to stay in one place because the	27
wind pushed me from here to there. It was	36
like being a yo-yo on a string, going back	45
and forth. Each time I thought I was safe,	54
another gust blew me off in another direction.	62
My friends were trying to play kickball, but	70
the ball kept blowing away. It was like a	79
funny movie.	81
The teachers were not happy, either. They	88
were all together in a bunch, trying to keep	97
their hair neat. Mr. Lewis wasn't with the other	106
teachers; he was pushing the girls on the	114
swings. It was an easy job since the wind did	124
most of the work.	128
My sister was out at recess, too. She and	137
her friend Mary were trying to write a play but	147
their papers kept blowing away. I tried to help	156
her catch them, but it was hard. We got all	166
the pieces, so we didn't litter, but the pages	175
were ruined. My sister and Mary decided to	183
chase me instead of writing, and we had a	192
great time. We were blown from here to there	201
and it was fun.	205

Word Count – 205

Scoring

Word recognition accuracy:

$$\frac{\text{Words correct}}{\text{Total words read orally}} = \underline{\hspace{2cm}} = \underline{\hspace{2cm}} \%$$

Fluency-Automaticity: _____ wcpm

Multidimensional Fluency Scale

Expression and Volume: _____

Phrasing and Intonation: _____

Smoothness: _____

Pace: _____

Total Score: _____

Comprehension: _____

Comments and Observations:

My teacher, Mrs. Quinn, is awesome. I think she deserves an award for teaching. I have liked all my teachers, but she is absolutely the best teacher I've ever had. Mrs. Quinn has long, brown, curly hair, and she smiles a lot. I even like the sound of her voice; it's almost musical. When I look at her, it always makes me happy. She wears pretty dresses that flow around her ankles like water.

Mrs. Quinn is nearly always nice. Learning with Mrs. Quinn is always enjoyable. She lets us work with buddies, and we can make noise as long as it is "good noise." Mrs. Quinn gives us homework every day. She says we need to show our homework to our parents so we can teach them, too. She says teaching someone else is the best way to learn something.

Mrs. Quinn does not like it when people are mean to each other. She sends the mean person a look that you know means trouble. Then she smiles at the other person. She doesn't say anything right away, but you know she will. The rest of the day is spent worrying what she will do, but people who behave well and do their work don't have to worry. Being in Mrs. Quinn's class is always an adventure. I hope I have more teachers like her.

Name of student _____ Date of testing _____

Grade 3: Form D

My teacher, Mrs. Quinn, is awesome. I	7
think she deserves an award for teaching. I	15
have liked all my teachers, but she is	23
absolutely the best teacher I've ever had.	30
Mrs. Quinn has long, brown, curly hair, and she	39
smiles a lot. I even like the sound of her voice;	50
it's almost musical. When I look at her, it	59
always makes me happy. She wears pretty	66
dresses that flow around her ankles like water.	74
Mrs. Quinn is nearly always nice. Learning	81
with Mrs. Quinn is always enjoyable. She lets us	90
work with buddies, and we can make noise as	99
long as it is "good noise." Mrs. Quinn gives us	109
homework every day. She says we need to	117
show our homework to our parents so we can	126
teach them, too. She says teaching someone	133
else is the best way to learn something.	141
Mrs. Quinn does not like it when people	149
are mean to each other. She sends the mean	158
person a look that you know means trouble.	166
Then she smiles at the other person. She	174
doesn't say anything right away, but you	181
know she will. The rest of the day is spent	191
worrying what she will do, but people who	199
behave well and do their work don't have	207
to worry. Being in Mrs. Quinn's class is always	216
an adventure. I hope I have more teachers	224
like her.	226

Word Count – 226

Scoring

Word recognition accuracy:

$$\frac{\text{Words correct}}{\text{Total words read orally}} = \underline{\hspace{1.5cm}} = \underline{\hspace{1.5cm}} \%$$

Fluency-Automaticity: _____ wcpm

Multidimensional Fluency Scale

Expression and Volume: _____

Phrasing and Intonation: _____

Smoothness: _____

Pace: _____

Total Score: _____

Comprehension: _____

Comments and Observations:

Test Passages

GRADE 4 BOOKLET:

Student Passages and Teacher Pages

Family trips are important to my parents, so we go lots of places together. Saturday we went to an art museum in the city. It was a beautiful building. Since huge stones covered the steps to get inside, it felt like walking through a tunnel. The front door was so big an elephant could have fit through it. It was an exciting walk just to get in.

We saw a medieval exhibit. We studied this period in school, so I knew a lot about it. The first room was filled with suits of armor. There were all kinds; some I had not seen before. My mother said the room was like a store for knights. My favorite suit of armor looked like one I had seen in a book. It was silver, shiny, and it was made to cover the whole body. It made me think of a haunted house and how people sometimes hide in armor to scare you.

Then we went into a room of paintings from that time period. They were nice. The museum was very quiet when we were there. It reminded me of the library at school. There were lots more rooms in the exhibit. We went to almost all of them. The armor room was my favorite, though.

Name of student _____ Date of testing _____

Grade 4: Form A

Family trips are important to my parents, so we	9
go lots of places together. Saturday we went to an	19
art museum in the city. It was a beautiful building.	29
Since huge stones covered the steps to get inside, it	39
felt like walking through a tunnel. The front door was	49
so big an elephant could have fit through it. It was	60
an exciting walk just to get in.	67
We saw a medieval exhibit. We studied this	75
period in school, so I knew a lot about it. The first	87
room was filled with suits of armor. There were all	97
kinds; some I had not seen before. My mother said	107
the room was like a store for knights. My favorite suit	118
of armor looked like one I had seen in a book. It was	131
silver, shiny, and it was made to cover the whole	141
body. It made me think of a haunted house and	151
how people sometimes hide in armor to scare you.	160
Then we went into a room of paintings from that	170
time period. They were nice. The museum was very	179
quiet when we were there. It reminded me of the	189
library at school. There were lots more rooms in the	199
exhibit. We went to almost all of them. The armor	209
room was my favorite, though.	214

Word Count – 214

Scoring

Word recognition accuracy:

$$\frac{\text{Words correct}}{\text{Total words read orally}} = \underline{\hspace{2cm}} = \underline{\hspace{1.5cm}} \%$$

Fluency-Automaticity: _____ wcpm

Multidimensional Fluency Scale

Expression and Volume: _____

Phrasing and Intonation: _____

Smoothness: _____

Pace: _____

Total Score: _____

Comprehension: _____

Comments and Observations:

Pizza is absolutely my favorite food. If I could, I would eat it every day for breakfast, lunch, and dinner. I would eat it inside or outside, at home or at school. I just love it; each and every pizza makes my mouth water.

A good crust is baked just right, not too hard and not too soft. The dough is tossed high into the air like a ball being bounced by a seal. It is a perfect circle just waiting for cheese, sauce, and other good things. The sauce is red like a superhero's cape. The taste makes your tongue leap up and do a little dance.

My favorite part is the cheese. The cheese on pizza should be thick and gooey. It pulls from your mouth like taffy. It sticks to your face like cotton candy. I like to have so much it slides off the crust like a waterfall when you pick up each slice. All together these tastes make the most wonderful food in the world, pizza.

Name of student _____   Date of testing _____

Grade 4: Form B

Pizza is absolutely my favorite food. If I could, I	10
would eat it every day for breakfast, lunch, and	19
dinner. I would eat it inside or outside, at home or at	31
school. I just love it; each and every pizza makes my	42
mouth water.	44
A good crust is baked just right, not too hard	54
and not too soft. The dough is tossed high into the air	66
like a ball being bounced by a seal. It is a perfect	78
circle just waiting for cheese, sauce, and other good	87
things. The sauce is red like a superhero's cape. The	97
taste makes your tongue leap up and do a little	107
dance.	108
My favorite part is the cheese. The cheese on	117
pizza should be thick and gooey. It pulls from your	127
mouth like taffy. It sticks to your face like cotton	137
candy. I like to have so much it slides off the crust like	150
a waterfall when you pick up each slice. All together	160
these tastes make the most wonderful food in the	169
world, pizza.	171

Word Count – 171

Scoring

Word recognition accuracy:

$$\frac{\text{Words correct}}{\text{Total words read orally}} = \underline{\qquad} = \underline{\qquad} \%$$

Fluency-Automaticity: _____ wcpm

Multidimensional Fluency Scale

  Expression and Volume: _____

  Phrasing and Intonation: _____

  Smoothness: _____

  Pace: _____

  Total Score: _____

Comprehension: _____

Comments and Observations:

Today is a dark and rainy day. It has been raining since I woke up. It rained all day at school, and it rained the whole way home on the bus. It rained as I walked home from the bus stop, and it is still raining now. Outside, water covers the ground. It is like the whole world has turned into a swimming pool that is just deep enough to come up to your ankles.

Leaves cover all the lawns and streets. They have been ripped from their branches by raindrops that have been falling endlessly, taking with them everything in their path. The leaves almost seem to be wondering what they did to deserve this; it wasn't their time to fall yet.

Cars drive by with their headlights on, even though it is daytime. The sun is gone, and I wonder when it will come back. I sit by my window waiting for the rain to stop. I hope it stops soon. Winter is coming; I need to be outside playing every day before the cold comes. Today is a dark and rainy day. It has been raining ever since I woke up.

Name of student _____ Date of testing _____

Grade 4: Form C

Today is a dark and rainy day. It has been	10
raining since I woke up. It rained all day at school,	21
and it rained the whole way home on the bus. It	32
rained as I walked home from the bus stop, and it is	44
still raining now. Outside, water covers the ground. It	53
is like the whole world has turned into a swimming	63
pool that is just deep enough to come up to your	74
ankles.	75
Leaves cover all the lawns and streets. They	83
have been ripped from their branches by raindrops	91
that have been falling endlessly, taking with them	99
everything in their path. The leaves almost seem to	108
be wondering what they did to deserve this; it	117
wasn't their time to fall yet.	123
Cars drive by with their headlights on, even	131
though it is daytime. The sun is gone, and I wonder	142
when it will come back. I sit by my window waiting	153
for the rain to stop. I hope it stops soon. Winter is	165
coming; I need to be outside playing every day	174
before the cold comes. Today is a dark and rainy	184
day. It has been raining ever since I woke up.	194

Word Count — 194

Scoring

Word recognition accuracy:

$$\frac{\text{Words correct}}{\text{Total words read orally}} = \underline{\hspace{2cm}} = \underline{\hspace{2cm}} \%$$

Fluency-Automaticity: _____ wcpm

Multidimensional Fluency Scale

Expression and Volume: _____

Phrasing and Intonation: _____

Smoothness: _____

Pace: _____

Total Score: _____

Comprehension: _____

Comments and Observations:

My grandmother is the best person in the world. Going to her house is really fun. Every Sunday I visit her, and we do all the things that a grandma and grandson should. Once in a while I even sleep over.

My grandmother is old, but she doesn't look it. She is short and round and soft all over. When she hugs me, I feel like I am being wrapped in a cloud. Grandma always wears an apron; sometimes the apron is a bright color, and sometimes it is just plain white, but she always has one on. She even wears one in the morning when she makes me bacon.

Telling stories is the thing that my grandma does best. You always know when she is going to tell a story. Her eyes get dreamy and she sits back in the closest chair. When she tells a story, I feel like I am there. It is like I walked into the picture in her mind.

The best stories are the ones about when she was young and my grandfather was still alive. Grandpa died a few years ago. Her stories help me remember him. Grandma and Grandpa lived next door to each other when they were little. She says they were best friends from the start, like peas in a pod. Sometimes after Grandma tells a story about Grandpa, she looks a little sad. That is when I do something funny to cheer her up. She says I am more fun to watch than television. I am my grandma's best friend now; we are two peas in a pod.

Name of student _____ Date of testing _____

Grade 4: Form D

My grandmother is the best person in the world.	9
Going to her house is really fun. Every Sunday I visit	20
her, and we do all the things that a grandma and	31
grandson should. Once in a while I even sleep over.	41
My grandmother is old, but she doesn't look it.	50
She is short and round and soft all over. When she	61
hugs me, I feel like I am being wrapped in a cloud.	73
Grandma always wears an apron; sometimes the	80
apron is a bright color, and sometimes it is just plain	91
white, but she always has one on. She even wears	101
one in the morning when she makes me bacon.	110
Telling stories is the thing that my grandma does	119
best. You always know when she is going to tell a	130
story. Her eyes get dreamy and she sits back in the	141
closest chair. When she tells a story, I feel like I am	153
there. It is like I walked into the picture in her mind.	165
The best stories are the ones about when she	174
was young and my grandfather was still alive.	182
Grandpa died a few years ago. Her stories help me	192
remember him. Grandma and Grandpa lived next	199
door to each other when they were little. She says	209
they were best friends from the start, like peas in a	220
pod. Sometimes after Grandma tells a story about	228
Grandpa, she looks a little sad. That is when I do	239
something funny to cheer her up. She says I am more	250
fun to watch than television. I am my grandma's	259
best friend now; we are two peas in a pod.	269

Word Count – 269

Scoring

Word recognition accuracy:

$$\frac{\text{Words correct}}{\text{Total words read orally}} = \underline{\hspace{2cm}} = \underline{\hspace{1.5cm}} \%$$

Fluency-Automaticity: _____ wcpm

Multidimensional Fluency Scale

   Expression and Volume: _____

   Phrasing and Intonation: _____

   Smoothness: _____

   Pace: _____

   Total Score: _____

Comprehension: _____

Comments and Observations:

CLASS RECORD SHEET

Grade: _____

School Year: _____

Teacher: _____

Student Name	Date of Testing	Word Recognition Accuracy	Fluency-Automaticity (wcpm)	Multidimensional Fluency Scale	Expression and Volume	Phrasing and Intonation	Smoothness	Pace	Comprehension	Date of Testing	Word Recognition Accuracy	Fluency-Automaticity (wcpm)	Multidimensional Fluency Scale	Expression and Volume	Phrasing and Intonation	Smoothness	Pace	Comprehension	Date of Testing	Word Recognition Accuracy	Fluency-Automaticity (wcpm)	Multidimensional Fluency Scale	Expression and Volume	Phrasing and Intonation	Smoothness	Pace	Comprehension	Date of Testing	Word Recognition Accuracy	Fluency-Automaticity (wcpm)	Multidimensional Fluency Scale	Expression and Volume	Phrasing and Intonation	Smoothness	Pace	Comprehension

3-Minute Reading Assessments: Word Recognition, Fluency, and Comprehension—Grades 1–4 Scholastic Teaching Resources

INDIVIDUAL STUDENT RECORD SHEET

Teacher: _____ **Student:** _____ **Grade:** _____

School Year: _____

	Score		Comments
		Form A Date of Administration: _____	
Word Recognition Accuracy			
Fluency-Automaticity (wcpm)			
Multidimensional Fluency Scale			
Expression and Volume			
Phrasing and Intonation			
Smoothness			
Pace			
Comprehension			
		Form B Date of Administration: _____	
Word Recognition Accuracy			
Fluency-Automaticity (wcpm)			
Multidimensional Fluency Scale			
Expression and Volume			
Phrasing and Intonation			
Smoothness			
Pace			
Comprehension			
		Form C Date of Administration: _____	
Word Recognition Accuracy			
Fluency-Automaticity (wcpm)			
Multidimensional Fluency Scale			
Expression and Volume			
Phrasing and Intonation			
Smoothness			
Pace			
Comprehension			
		Form D Date of Administration: _____	
Word Recognition Accuracy			
Fluency-Automaticity (wcpm)			
Multidimensional Fluency Scale			
Expression and Volume			
Phrasing and Intonation			
Smoothness			
Pace			
Comprehension			

ADMINISTRATION AND SCORING AIDS

Word Recognition Accuracy (Decoding)

Divide the total number of words read correctly by the total number of words read (correct and incorrect). For example, if the student read a total of 94 words in the 60- second reading and made 8 errors, the percentage of words read correctly would be reflected in the following fraction:

$\frac{86}{94}$ (86 divided by 94) = 91.5% of words read correctly

Instructional reading level: 92–98%.
Independent reading level: 99–100%.

Reading Fluency-Automaticity

Count the number of words the student has read correctly during the 60-second oral reading. Words read correctly include those initially misread but corrected by the student. Use this chart to interpret results.

Grade	Fall wcpm*	Winter wcpm	Spring wcpm
1	0–10	10–50	30–90
2	30–80	50–100	70–130
3	50–110	70–120	80–140
4	70–120	80–130	90–140
5	80–130	90–140	100–150
6	90–140	100–150	110–160
7	100–150	110–160	120–170
8	110–160	120–180	130–180

*wcpm=words correct per minute

Comprehension

After the student has completed the 60-second oral reading and after you have read the entire passage to the student, remove the passage from view. Ask for a retelling of what he or she remembers. Next, ask if there is anything else the student can recall from the passage. If he or she is unable or unwilling to retell anything, you may probe for specific information (e.g., "What is the main idea of this story?"). When the student has told you as much as he or she can remember from the passage, rate the recall on the Comprehension Rubric.

○ Student has no recall or minimal recall of only a fact or two from the passage. **Rating Score: 1**

○ Student recalls a number of unrelated facts of varied importance. **Rating Score: 2**

○ Student recalls the main idea of the passage with a few supporting details. **Rating Score: 3**

○ Student recalls the main idea along with a fairly robust set of supporting details, although not necessarily organized logically or sequentially as presented in the passage. **Rating Score: 4**

○ Student recall is a comprehensive summary of the passage, presented in a logical order and/or with a robust set of details, and includes a statement of main idea. **Rating Score: 5**

○ Student recall is a comprehensive summary of the passage, presented in a logical order and/or with a robust set of details, and includes a statement of main idea. Student also makes reasonable connections beyond the text to his/her own personal life, another text, etc. **Rating Score: 6**

Reading Fluency-Expression

Listen to the student's 60-second oral reading. Rate it on the Multidimensional Fluency Scale.

Rating	Expression & Volume	Phrasing and Intonation	Smoothness	Pace
Circle one →	1 2 3 4	1 2 3 4	1 2 3 4	1 2 3 4
1	Reads words as if simply to get them out. Little sense of trying to make text sound like natural language. Tends to read in a quiet voice.	Reads in monotone with little sense of phrase boundaries; frequently reads word-by-word.	Makes frequent extended pauses, hesitations, false starts, sound-outs, repetitions, and/or multiple attempts.	Reads slowly and laboriously.
2	Begins to use voice to make text sound like natural language in some areas but not in others. Focus remains largely on pronouncing the words. Still reads in a quiet voice.	Frequently reads in two- and three-word phrases, giving the impression of choppy reading; improper stress and intonation fail to mark ends of sentences and clauses.	Experiences several "rough spots" in text where extended pauses or hesitations are more frequent and disruptive.	Reads moderately slowly or too quickly.
3	Makes text sound like natural language throughout the better part of the passage. Occasionally slips into expressionless reading. Voice volume is generally appropriate throughout the text.	Reads with a mixture of run-ons, mid-sentence pauses for breath, and some choppiness; reasonable stress and intonation.	Occasionally breaks smooth rhythm because of difficulties with specific words and/or structures.	Reads with an uneven mixture of fast and slow pace.
4	Reads with good expression and enthusiasm throughout the text. Varies expression and volume to match his or her interpretation of the passage.	Generally reads with good phrasing, mostly in clause and sentence units.	Generally reads smoothly with some breaks, but resolves word and structure difficulties quickly, usually through self-correction.	Consistently reads at conversational pace; appropriate rate throughout reading.

* This scale is an adaptation of one developed by Zutell & Rasinski, 1991. Kimberly Monfort, a third-grade teacher at Bon View School in Ontario, California developed the format above for the scale.

Total Score: _____

Instructional Ideas for Word Recognition, Fluency, and Comprehension

Word Recognition Instruction

For students experiencing difficulty in word recognition (percentage accuracy 90% or less while reading a grade-level passage), consider the following instructional ideas:

◇ Teach high-frequency words—for example, the Dolch List and the Fry Instant Word List. Teach five words a week, and practice them daily. Put the words on the word wall, and review the word wall each day. Play games with the words. Have students write the words while saying and spelling them.

◇ Teach common word families (phonograms or rimes—for example, -at in cat and bat). List and practice words belonging to the word family. Read poetry and other texts that contain the targeted word families. Have students write their own poems using words belonging to a word family. Add words studied from the word families to the classroom word wall.

◇ Have students sort words from the word wall or from some other source of words by various categories—by a particular vowel or consonant sound, by grammatical category, by some meaningful attribute of the word, and so on.

◇ Use flash cards and other practice activities for words under study. Keep these activities game-like and brief—no more than 5–10 minutes—and conduct them once or twice per day.

◇ Engage in word-building activities such as Making Words or Making and Writing Words. Provide students with a limited set of letters and guide them through the process of building (writing) words using those letters. Draw students' attention to the meaning, sound, and spelling of the words.

◇ Teach students to decode multisyllabic words. Teach basic syllabication rules (for example, in words with two vowels that are separated by one consonant, the word is normally divided into syllables after the first vowel [*hotel, legal, final*]; syllables that end in a vowel usually have the long vowel sound [*secret, baby, pilot*]).

◇ Help students detect prefixes, suffixes, and base words in longer words (for example, *replay, cowboy, basement*). Teach students how breaking larger words into prefixes, suffixes, and base words can help them to decode the larger word and determine its meaning.

◇ Use the cloze procedure to teach contextual word recognition. Find an appropriate text and delete words that can be determined from the context. Have students read the text with the deleted words and determine the missing words using the contextual information in the passage.

◇ Engage students in occasional conversations about *how* they decode unfamiliar words. During this work on self-monitoring, focus on confirmation as well by asking questions such as "How did you know you were right?"

◆ Encourage students to read at home and to practice words at home as well as in school.

◆ Engage students in games and game-like activities, such as word-based Wheel of Fortune, Go Fish, Concentration, and Wordo (word bingo) that give them the opportunity to practice the words they are studying.

◆ Use the fluency-building activities listed on the following pages to build word recognition skills as well as overall reading fluency.

◆ Provide students with plenty of opportunities to read texts that contain words they are studying.

◆ Develop a daily instructional routine (20–30 minutes) devoted to the various activities described in this section. Use some of the activities in this section in a systematic and regular way with students who are experiencing difficulty in learning to decode words.

Fluency Instruction

For students experiencing difficulty in reading fluency (reading rate less than the accepted norms while reading a grade-level passage), consider the following instructional ideas:

◆ Read to students on a regular basis. As you do so, be sure to model for them what fluent reading is like. Ask them to listen for the way you use your voice to convey meaning. If the students have a copy of the text you are reading, have them follow along silently while you read to them.

◆ Have individual students read a passage aloud while listening to you or another reader read with them. This is known as "assisted [paired] reading." The combination of a student's reading a text while listening to someone else read it fluently is a well-known means of improving fluency and comprehension. Make this a daily 10–15 minute routine. If no one is available to read with the student, record the reading on tape and have the student read the passage while listening to it on tape.

◆ Develop a daily home routine in which a parent sits side by side with the child and engages in assisted reading with the child for 10–15 minutes. If parents are not available, students may read while listening to a recorded version of the passage.

◆ Have students practice reading a passage (100–250 words in length) several times until they are able to read it accurately, quickly, and expressively. This technique, known as "repeated [practice] reading," may require 7 or 8 readings. The practice may occur over a period of several days and may be done at home as well as in school. Make this a daily classroom activity; once students have mastered one passage, have them move on to other equally or more challenging passages. Passages that are meant to be performed (for example, poetry, scripts, speeches) work very well to promote practiced and expressive reading.

◆ Combine repeated and assisted reading. Have students practice reading a passage several times until they are able to read it fluently. In addition to practicing the passage independently, students may also practice the passage while listening to a partner read it with them or while listening to a recorded version of the passage.

◆ Develop integrated fluency instructional routines—daily routines for fostering fluency that combine modeling, assisted reading, and repeated readings. The Fluency Development Lesson, described below, is one example of an integrated fluency routine.

- ◎ Work with a daily passage of 100–250 words that lends itself to expressive and interpretive reading. Make two copies of the passage for every student in the group.

- ◎ Read the passage to students several times while they follow along. Discuss the passage with students.

- ◎ Read the passage chorally several times with students.

- ◎ Next, have students work in pairs. Ideally, each pair should have its own quiet place in which to work. Have one student read the passage two or three times while the partner follows along silently and provides assistance when necessary. When the first reader has finished, the partners switch roles and repeat the process.

- ◎ Have student pairs perform their passage for their classmates or other audiences.

- ◎ Select interesting words from the passage and add them to the word wall for further practice, sorting, and use in writing.

- ◎ Place one copy of the passage into students' fluency folders for future practice. Send the other copy home for additional practice with parents.

- ◎ The following morning, begin by having students read the passage from the previous day. Then, begin a new lesson with a new passage.

◆ Provide students with daily time (15–20 minutes) for independent reading. Ensure that students read material that is at their independent reading level. Make students accountable for their independent reading time by having them summarize their daily reading in a reading journal. Alternately, you might have students read aloud (in a soft voice) during the independent reading period so that you can be assured they are actually reading the text.

Comprehension Instruction

For students experiencing difficulty in comprehension (retelling rated in the lower range on the comprehension rubric while reading a grade-level passage), consider the following instructional ideas:

◆ Before asking students to read a passage, ensure that they have sufficient background knowledge. You may increase background knowledge in a variety of ways:

- ◎ Provide information to students by telling them directly.

- ◎ Brainstorm background information with students.

- ◎ Read related material to students that will increase background knowledge.

- Use other print and non-print media such as movies, videotapes, the Internet, artifacts (for example, maps, music, food) to expand background knowledge.

- Bring in others who are knowledgeable about a topic to share information and personal experience with students.

◆ Use text maps or graphics with students. Present students with a text map or graphic that demonstrates the organization of the main ideas in a passage. This can be done before reading a passage. Alternately, give students a partially completed map or graphic to complete while they are reading a passage. Or provide an empty graphic for students and ask them to use it to make notes while they read.

◆ Once students are familiar with the idea of text maps and graphics, ask them to develop their own maps or graphics after reading a passage. The map or graphic should reflect the meaning of the passage and the overall organization of the ideas in the text.

◆ After reading a passage together, engage students in a lively discussion about it. Make sure the discussion goes beyond recitation of information contained in the passage. Encourage students to make reasoned inferences about the passage. Ask them to share opinions and ideas, always reminding them to provide justification for their assertions.

◆ Engage students in making predictions or hypotheses about what will happen next as they read. Ask them to justify their predictions and use the predictions as the basis for discussion of the passage with others.

◆ Ask students to develop relevant questions related to the passage before, during, and after reading it. Use these questions to guide discussion of the material.

◆ Select texts that lend themselves to image creation and encourage students to create images while they read these texts. Images can be internal mental images or actual drawings students make during and after reading. Have students use the images as a starting point for discussing the passage with others.

◆ Instruct students to take written notes (along with insights, observations, wonderings, and questions) while reading a passage, trying to capture in their notes the important ideas that are presented in the text. After reading and taking notes, students should use the notes to write a summary of the passage. Tell students to refer to their notes when discussing the passage.

◆ Encourage students to react to their reading by writing in journals or learning logs. Entries can be general reactions or focused responses (for example, favorite character, most important idea, most interesting part). For expository text, ask students to make log entries describing new processes or providing definitions of important concepts.

◆ Allow students to respond to a reading (re-represent the main ideas of a passage) in creative ways. These include:

- creating tableaux (performances of a passage in which students assume different stances, keeping their bodies motionless, to portray the essential meaning),